A FONDNESS FOR

C000261075

Charlie Baylis is from Nottingham, England. He is the editor of Anthropocene. His poetry has been nominated three times for the Pushcart Prize and once for the Forward Prize. This is his first collection of poetry. He spends his spare time completely adrift of reality.

ISBN: 978-1-915760-18-0

Cover designed by Aaron Kent

Edited & Typeset by Aaron Kent

Broken Sleep Books Ltd
Rhydwen
Talgarreg
Ceredigion
SA44 4HB

Broken Sleep Books Ltd
Fair View
St Georges Road
Cornwall
PL26 7YH

a fondness for the colour green

Charlie Baylis

Also by Charlie Baylis

Santa Lucía (Invisible Hand Press, 2021)

Swimming (Red Ceiling Press, 2019)

At First it Felt like Flying w/Andrew Taylor (Indigo Dreams, 2019)

Drag City (Broken Sleep Books, 2018)

Hilda Doolittle's Carl Jung T-Shirt (Erbacce Press, 2016)

Elizabeth (Agave Press, 2015)

Contents

this book is dedicated
to anybody who wants to escape

zero gravity

a homeless man listening to turbo-folk on the back of an asteroid
wearing a tunic of heather & vertigo   crumpled horizons
the fixed stars on his bike melt in the blizzard
he offers me a coin   stay a little longer

take these happiness pills for your green stones
take a little solace in your lemonade
take the slow sun glossing the brass tips of grass
take the memory of a poet who used to be holy
unfold in these rainbows

his hair is pinned to the back of his hands
wasps leaving prints on the yellow & black wind
he sits alone in an ice-cream parlour by the sea

here is an alternative path to the upside down
in eighteen days   you will remember nothing

i. an interest in symmetry

hi...

now that we're friends i will tell you about the buttercup,
china, the dragon & the fire eater, my glass of lemonade.
why are you standing at the traffic light when the light is green.
confused or worse, let's stay friends. come, i want to show you
the beautiful jazz of the sea. orphans asleep under pink rain -
destiny - do not wake the new world until the new world is ready
i want to plant these orange trees with these orange seeds
i want to raise a palace of tender hearts, hearts that are ours
but not ours. parents: don't ask -
we're dancing on the breeze the butterflies are born.

charlie wave

ANTI the letters that comprise the opening line
ANTI patterns of silk on a handful of silk
ANTI light of tangerine sunset on tangerine pool
ANTI the fourth line being absent of hook
ANTI fresh fruit fed to rotten children
ANTI philosophers at the window
ANTI hi…
ANTI plastic sun   ANTI   virgin moon
ANTI your grandmother shopping for a suit in tesco
ANTI spasmodic basement dancers electrifying a fawn
ANTI vegetating mid-career poets peeing onto mirrors
ANTI orange salad served by romans in space glasses
ANTI self immolation by nuns
   fight them with your claws   sisters !
ANTI adam the egg & eve the egg layer
ANTI vladimir putin stroking pandas in the satanic zoo
ANTI lesbian exploitation of lesbians drowning in laudanum
ANTI binary love song eating non binary code
ANTI that you have stopped reading
ANTI 'charlie wave' sung by rihanna   madonna   hannah arendt
ANTI *any* person of voice & style more beautiful than charlie
ANTI swirl of neon in black hole caffeine glitch   ANTI nothing
ANTI ow!
ANTI brunch with juliet binoche without a top hat
ANTI you   ANTI your nightmares   ANTI your awful frock
ANTI your god-awful taste
ANTI the tears glittering in your beard
ANTI everything that has come
ANTI everything that will follow

ANTI everything that shares the truth of ANTI
ANTI charlie wave   but not
ANTI the dolphins riding the happy seas
ANTI letters that do not comprise the final line

PRO charlie

i'm still looking for the perfect lover

for julia

it's like when you're on you're completely on
running for the door
pissing for the camera
new york is not as young as she was & besides
life can be pretty unbearable
but who cares for the dingy passages of the subway
when we can throw all the wine glasses in washington heights
from the window to the wall
& feel like
favourite records on swing sets
lovers tonguing in a foreign language
charlie charms & poems
wait a sec
julia
you may never become the painter you dreamt of becoming
but somewhere a lonely boy is picking apples
beneath the beautiful lights of the lower east side
      & you see yourself
the moment you tense for the sweetness of the apple
an ocean baptises a new ocean
      one drink
      two drinks
      hallelujah!

lose your illusion

the moon is a little bitch
— hera lindsay bird

hera told me "happiness is a monochrome kite
blowing in a cartoon breeze"
an illusion to lose scrawled on the back of a postcard
inaccurately stamped & addressed to the wrong ex

tearing down sunset boulevard
where the window blinds are lit by gorgeous light
the boats in the harbour twinkle with soft french verbs

she told me it can be hard to hold on to an illusion
when words grow scarce
soon as we try

she smiled
           she never waved good-bye

w else can i tell you about mermaids u don't already know

a voice in white that you can't really hear
coming up for air whispering
i like you but i am not sure
we share very little move closer
(the title is from an interview with luna miguel
i just bought her book about mermaids
after not being sure for a long time
whether or not i would like her book about mermaids
if someone is very popular or part of a movement
it is easy to doubt their sincerity)
i would say you are worth many florins
you go swimming in the pools of famous gardens
you arrive home late & then go to sleep
i have so many questions for you

far out

for serge Ψ neptune

when i was a boy i found it hard to breathe
there were many things with which i disagreed

i tried not to take my sadness seriously
i tried to wear it lightly
they were just feelings
immaterial
memories of the atlantic burning
seagulls circling the bay
the wild beneath the waves

i slipped my bandages
started to feel comfortable in my skin
took cold baths
ate mussels oysters scallops fine cuts of dolphin meat
my hair grew tangled & waved
i swam far out

everything was beautiful

dystopia

in memory of sean bonney

the eagle with gold bars melting in her mind
lava over the opal mines
ashes in a bucket of ice-cream
the silkworm eating herself tail to mouth
at the centre of a roundabout is hope
philosophers gridlocked in philadelphia
eagles dropping bars of gold over opal mines
between you & me sean bonney
i've had enough of this shit
nothing everyone & nobody
the city is killing me
the city hates my poetry
the city is a fucking nightmare
sean bonney do not fear
we will bury the dystopia
in unreadable film scripts under the pyramids
empty space expanding into empty space
your heart beating at the centre of the earth
bluebells growing green in the belly of bluewhales
black banners in riots for peace
re capitalism: fuck you
golden snow dropping gently over the opal mines
the sun is one of seven stars
rays of light polish our nightmares
write to me when the war is over
write to me when we have won

madonna

there's no art in america, it's all sugar & war.
— sophie robinson

i wake up dreaming i've made it
here in new york   i've made it   everywhere
dreaming of myself as a cheerleader
the tassels of my glittering pom-poms are unblemished lines of philosophy
the blue sky shines & shades through blinds
the blue sky is grace kelly's eyes
in my bed there is no art but sugar & war adorn rhetorical walls
& maybe i can tell you a secret about the strength of the bedposts
& maybe i can't
at the heart of sophie's poem is sadness
the still water below which the poem sinks
is sadness
nothing hurts more than loving somebody who doesn't love you

one film ends & another film begins
but it is the same film
wrapped up in the rhetorical walls we walk through
i notice a picture of a poet eating breakfast in berlin
the summer before he died
i think of their curious friendship
the music of his voice burning holes in the ceiling
the music of her voice burning holes in the ceiling
i think of sunny days kayaking down the hudson
into the arms of another new york to the one you knew
where partisans are gathering butterflies
along the meadows of the highway
beneath the beautiful lights of the lower east side

today offers a fraction of what won't be returned tomorrow
the branches which held suicides are full of life

green & yellow leaves jangling in the sun
canaries carrying the ocean in their beaks
will find a new river
once one evaporates   into the clouds of grace kelly's eyes
this is the part where you arrive home & close the door
blow out every candle on the cake
turn out the lights
& everything is forgotten

ii. spilling pink champagne on your party dress

pink champagne at the pony club

the second step was a rose blossoming
under impure light, paper tablecloth,
image of drowned bee; a galaxy born

in the hollow of a spoon, the nun i loved
loved a number of nuns. told me,
the bible was a prose poem for the moon.

i wept ribbons onto her jaguar.
on the racecourse i drank
pink champagne at the pony club,

jesuits ripped the radio up, a girl
gave me a daisy chain that went on forever,

balled over to me in leather boots,
put my foot through the table, since then
i've been trying to stay in the now.

hilda doolittle's carl jung t-shirt

hilda, i have many thoughts of you,
the little that you do, you do, you do.
the grass burns on a knoll in berlin,
there are cheerleaders kissing in soft core,

soft pom-poms, soft 32 dimensions.
where is the pear in your purple heart?
you send blank roses, your legs are a fallacy,
your dark eyes shine like an apocalypse.

you are mother mary & sister ray.
i lost my oyster card in an octopus's garden
in the shade, all the hens stumble sideways
& i can't remember the next line.

*

hilda, can we move somewhere with better taste?
the bright lights are confusing baby turtles.
the rocket in my salad might punish the atom.
kiss me — all your vowels pound with sound

but your features are isometric: *jung forever*
is the legend on your t shirt, a semi-literate joke,
but i don't want to stare for fear i'll offend you

as you may think i'm looking at your breasts
which i am but i don't mean to, hilda, if i apologize:
it's not that i'm sorry, it's that i think i should be sorry.

rebecca

is a comet   she collides with a poem
about the realist movement in italian cinema
i get it   i think there were many great films

rebecca tastes of the beach at midnight   i
watch wave by wave wave by in the green of her eyes
rebecca is not a comet

rebecca works in a sweetshop   drips light
onto reels   her passion for pearl is peach   she says
pistachio always tastes like the moon

k

for aaron kent

head of k dripping with jewels
coke stain on ceiling
cracks in our bedroom black

k we've reached the cap
pain disintegrates in freckles
butterflies painted

on the darkest night
undress me
pepper me with pepper

k rides the northern line lip
sweet like an unexploded cherry bomb
sperm spumes up my spine

i think of the holy ghost

autumn in kyoto

green fruit pastilles &
        houellebecq

huge acacias
powdering out the sunset

                rejection
                  all the sad girls
                      in kasumi pearls

singer-sargent
  &
submarines   gashed lungs

  south-rushing waterfalls
opium clouds rashed by lantern light

ophelia face down
        in deep oceans of milk

        in the rear-view mirror
i glimpse her
  loveless in kyoto

okinawa

around the corner from the refinery
a red lighthouse dances with a green lighthouse
in the ballroom

i gave my sandals to the sea
you said stop
pull the reign over

me, a silent spirit
lost on the ocean path
a shadow spent over water

the black boat burns
you walk the ruins with me
across the old country

i take you
smoke spirals
from the napalm grass

i can only stand so much
of the waves' delicacy
thirteen villas, one empty

sixty-four steps to the sea
then back
sixty four steps of radiant green

the orphan draped in expensive rags (gun in hand)
the promise of hypnotic beauty
the torpedo gathering momentum

a golden strand of hair on the sand
or the foam print pattern
on your back, tensed

heavy air
bullets a vortex
in a shell

i am not interested in symmetry
the moment has passed

ghosts in the back whacked out soldiers
green grapes & cigarettes
an outstretched palm

you are no longer
i am no longer
who we want to be

night moves

small pieces of wing washed up along the shore
branches of sleep strung with starflowers
satchels of dreams protected by thieves
if you know who you are
know who you are
who you are

the long candle casts pools of light over the bedroom floor
oceanic light where ships are sinking
night is so heavy
it will take cranes to lift her
beyond the door

new worlds are opening in the hum of distant spheres
the owls carry petty crimes in their feathers, pray
what good would it do?
why are you running away?
why are you running away from me?

iii. so you think you're in love with jennifer

jennysis

one night in middlesex
reading phillipson's *instant-flex*   professor jex
pulled apart the loaves of a lady s legs

one night in middlesex   reading teletext
toy plane lodged in anus   the speed blurred
along an airfield   he waved goodbye

oooo' s when the images tripled in the image teller's telex
aaaah' s when the plasma trembled in the beautiful womb
oooo' s when out popped jenny x   ravaged with life

her mother dead   he scrawled an x on her felt tip head

not knowing the gender at her apex
flipped a coin   became the stronger sex   xy not xx   miss
red jenny's first word in read:

j e n x

jenny comes glittering with metropolis
her star bright knickers eclipse the bright star

jenny comes with a swastika tattooed to her thigh
[the sign made by reeds   as seen in hinduism

buddism   jainism]   isn't it ironic   jenny   this rain
on your wedding day   no it's not
the green light beneath a copyright sign

i used to long for you jenny   when you were a mushroom
spooring in psychedelic space

i used to long for you jenny   when you were a holy poet
now you are a hat stand

& when i told you   *i love you*
i did not mean i love you

raymond carver s rasberry fetish

the last time i saw raymond carver
      he was ogling goggles or goggling oggles
off his tits   somewhere in eastphalia

or westphalia i
asked raymond what he thought of my poem

s*o you*
think you're in love
with jennifer

he told me it wasn't worth the paper it was written on

i said   damn my ancient gold edged bible
         parchment   four inch deep ivory cut   spine
         byron jizzed on my mum's mum's mum's mum's

mum
he told me i was an imbecile
   i bowed deeply

taking coffee with charlie baylis

this poem was written by juliette binoche

juliette binoche typed me this poem topless
she told me of an illusion: a hamburger
that is just a hamburger flavoured hamburger

i write better with my tongue tied in leather
i write better with my tongue dipped in lime
i have googled myself sixteen times today
but no one has commented on the colour of my tongue

juliette binoche licked a razor-blade & the world fell apart
i rolled down the esplanade with flip-flops under my feet
i googled myself thirty-two times today
but no one has commented on the flip-flops

under my feet   my tongue dipped in lime &
juliette binoche   i am afraid of my self-obsession
    i am afraid i might start to enjoy myself

the turn in the sonnet

one night in middlesex   next
one night in sunny bethlehem   tex

whales dabbing in the ocean green
smoke coming out my breath   next   thirty four years next

i d/l a picture from the internet
jenny with her ex   green vomit   on a cigarette

a piece of mashed potato drips from my copy of *instant-flex*
raymond carver eyeballs a raspberry   reveals

the turn in the sonnet usually comes in around line nine
or line ten   charlie   i'm so impressed
but what's all this shit about mash potata !?

so now i am jenny's ex
a million motherflipping nights in middlesex
i can t see the fog for the window

god i miss you jenny x

god i miss you jenny x
your pillow case soft with self consciousness
alphabet light illuminating motes of dust on your window

god i miss you jenny x
the hippy tattooing the swastika to your thigh
the leather almonds melting in space

where will you go jenny   what will you do
once you were a holy poet   now you are a hat stand
once you peed on pelicans   pen dipped in the pacific
once you graffitied granada with gold garcia-lorca eye-liner

now i cannot name what swirls inside you   now i cannot hold you
these lonely nights in middlesex   jenny good   jenny gone
in star bright knickers
she came glittering with metropolis

jenny wave

at 8 o clock jenny s green nails puncture my soft toy heart
    my little boy dreams   hot steam
rises from a cupcake   *forget it c h e r l I e it s not like*
you re getting anything from me   it s not like you re winning
it s not like anybody cares

i undress the colour green
she pins a spin inside her thigh
i listen as she begins

she tells me of the poets mating in the milky way
she tells me of peter pan pulling nails from pillows
    face down in a hotel bed
she tells me of phrasal verbs   phrasal verbs   for example
    get fucked

but nobody knows her name in mexico
nobody   not even tinkerbell
& tinkerbell hates jenny the same way i do

h e l l o k i t t y

jenny left for japan
  maybelline in her lashes   charlie in her eyes
her green wig   blew   beneath a blue chicago sky
maybe she was born with it

the stance she stood in called pretending
      the felt-tips she circled at the gates of hell   *maybe it was*
maybelline

i threw her zoo in the garbage   her spiders in the garage
        i didn't want to forget   i wanted to forget
the grammar of the axis   the zulus in the reeds

the lines she wrote   so   lunatic   loco
      a coconut without the coco   hello moto
hello yoko   go blow bubbles in the milkshakes of tokyo

go polish your poetry prize
does it keep you warm at night?

iv. an addiction to symmetry

stephanie says

for estefania cabello

for a long time you've been staring out into sea
holding a green door open with the tip of your toe
a door that leads to nowhere, nowhere we know.
the door might open to you,
depending on the angle from which you approach,
the weight of your dreams,
which seashell you are calling from.

you watch me from a distance with a mirror of cut glass
somewhere where the wind over wet sand whispers
but we do not know what the wind over wet sand whispers
anyway, it is not important.

i think of you holding the sea open with an outstretched arm
behaving like waves, the direction the door is moving.
when you are the door, when you are not the room.

it's clear you wouldn't return my call

                                      if i called.

it's clear i wouldn't return your call

                                      if you called.

what are you wearing?
do you still have the sunlight in your hair?
do you remember what stephanie says and where?
she's asking is it good or bad

small cities in belgium

excuse me, do you know who i am?
a spectacle rolls into my bowl of cornflakes
milk splashes the cover *famous peots of the 1980s*
the typo was my idea.
fuck it.
somewhere in the stuck-together-pages, lifted text & men in awful coats
my finger stumbles upon clive,
ah clive.
three men liked his pamphlet in 1985
three men though they were his friends
three men *because* they were his friends
we once toured the small cities of belgium. antwerp ant-
werp antwerp.
i can't talk, my mouth is full of waffle
i can write, mostly waffle
i'm so sorry i didn't quite catch your name
it sounded like charlie boredshitless

unica zürn

i see her in the distance
weighing the trees   their scales
searching for that found sound

a snowflake eluding the cat's eye
cloud-mouthed, throwing an arrow into space
'i need silence, don't touch me'

those were six of her words
the rest drift away

lana del rey

fake lashes flutter
over the perfect
prom date

i sink

she
dives into the ice cream
clouds

heartbeat
flickering

six by six   pink wig   slit wrists
it's all over now
baby blue

yesterday
stuck on repeat
swinging to the same beat

psychics in sunglasses
rewinding
heaven's atomic sunset

the shadow in the sunlight
with the west coast
under her wings

singing *hey*
that's no way
to say
goodbye

a + e

for emily

stay away from *my* sister, stay away from *my* soup.
life is easy when you live alone, my sister says.
she lives in a castle, chews sun like chewing gum.
do you like my sister? kiss her at the bus stop.
my nose is turning green. can't keep my eyes
off her, take her home. marry her to a frog,
if a blonde prince waits. know when to stop?
stop a second before she says stop
her bedroom window ripples to let rain in
each drop becomes larger in my mind.
broken into pieces by spies. you know my sister?
what is it you want with her?
amber spring showers. revolution is a recipe.
i can't win. a hole haunts my bathtub of gin.
when i was a boy i pretended to drown every time
my pearl toe green a swimming pool.
i want to sigh a kite.
for the past three nights i've been sleeping in a + e.
electricity has made a mess of me.
fold away my map of emily. i don't need her.
every face flickering
on my screen reminds me so sweetly of my sister,
the moment her hair spilled into yellow flowers.

a fondness for the colour green

stems from your addiction to symmetry.
we must leave the city before dogs
machine gun us to death.

against agatha. against bianca. in favour of charlie.
chelsea has been replaced by a cigar
shaped swimming pool

i think i saw you by the flume, rebecca, pretending to be a pear.
ed miliband was eating your pips.
the situation was delicate.

*

in spanish summers walk with the sun behind you.
the bikini defeated franco.
fascism is licking the wrong ice cream.

when eating a watermelon wear a parachute.
do not forget what is suggested by biting
pink flesh, green flesh, pink flesh.

in seville the most important square
was hoisted 30 foot in the air.
to make what was unimportant seem important.

there is a hole in my head
& it is tempting to conclude i've learnt nothing from you
except the loneliness of a sunday afternoon

with a perfect hand of playing cards
when all of the players have vanished.

green axolotls

these new paradigms
the graceful merlin   lands
in the palm   of   my   hands

rapping the glass   attracts   risk
     rapping harder   death threats   dream song spiralling in her dna
i hope she   i hope she   i hope she   ends   me

green bones   poisoned mice   prayers   to spoilt kids
     drawling   ink over felt veldt   violet vine
vvindowsills   [play v sense]   the cards lie face down

the security that glass attracts: amateur witchcraft   little armour
     green powder   &   strange   affections   the girl at my door

flowering like poetry on the underside of the night

revolutionary road

it was as it was, or as it were: queer
frank o'hara stepped out of a taxi in times square
lana turner dipped her pen in moon ink,
perched on the crescent moon:
so happy to see you here, new york
all the tender hearts beat in the underwater hotel,
laughing at the bible, laughing at death,
laughing at allen ginsberg
his shadow chained to the atlantic.
ken koch rode down-town on the 1 train.
no one in new york knew his name.
the main concern: bottled starfish,
sinatra spectacles, joan jett
bathing in the blue blood of every man she loved,
bernadette mayer in moscow, writing of teen
suicide in red-square
shades of green over the glittering sea,
the red ghosts of mccarthy.

it took a thousand years for anyone to say anything
it took a thousand more for anyone to add anything
meanwhile there are cracks where shoes appear.
& we just go on living,
watching the snow fall from our house on
revolutionary road. it was as it was,
or as it were: as before.

v. a bunch of idiots talking don delillo

roman holiday

wherever you go in rome you are only a stone's throw
from romans baked in bread or thrown from a stone
left of the spanish steps you will find the ursula le guin
pen monument take a left to the statue where sinatra slept
you may note the shoes i am in indicate a state of tension
come fuck me with nuclear weapons dripping from your neck
is a polite invitation to read novels at the foot of my bed
talk with me about don delillo until time flips left
i like the story where sinatra falls asleep inside a spoon
all of the lights go out & the future is orange

night flight

hey i just finished writing a poem called roman holiday
the poem is a polite invitation to saw my kitchen table in two
have you seen the film? it stars a young audrey hepburn
if you'd like to get in touch it's charlie_baylis@msn.com
perhaps you'd prefer to stick a spoon into don delillo's
novel sweep green trees from a bad angle
talk to me of the time sinatra slept beside the statue of a spoon
ten-thousand feet below bald men walk their dogs
round & round the foggy ruins of time
– can you see my boredom through the clouds?
if you can't reach me [charlie_baylis@msn.com]
try yumping off a cliff

sandals

i fell off my bike dreaming of you
cara delevingne
drenched in vanilla & shoegaze i get it
jacques villeneuve gliding mistletoe first into a bale of hay
charlie parker blowing brass in a crack pipe
my photons have become professional patience is
the art of looking backwards while moving
forwards into a small hole gravity circles
i hope to kiss you in the supermarket talk about the euro
till my desire is submerged in whipped cream
you won't really know what i mean till you know
what i mean hang tough do you know what

vandals

nous sommes la claque & vous êtes la joue

— robert desnos

sitting in yr garden dreaming of cable
every day is silent & grey
jumping off a cliff in a green sweater any questions
a penny for your photons a suitcase full of whipped cream
fresh supermarket on the train to gotham a gang of vandals
sat down left of my ego & sang me their phone numbers
my phone number is 0115 9621073 thank you cara delevingne
selena gomez raymond roussel fish nailed to sales i'm spinning
around move left my pockets are getting deeper
charlie parker hot pants peas & animé
the same joke repeated over & over
lips so sweet like
you are lucky your nose is still standing
you are lucky there is still some oxygen
left i am a camera

moonlight simile

riding on a bike while the bike falls apart
riding on a horse while the house falls apart
riding on a cart while the roman empire falls apart
i can't stop thinking about you
a tick on your twitter means you are deluded or genuinely famous
either way you've probably never seen the inside of a spoon
i can't understand why i am so "terribly unhappy"
i listen to songs consisting of the same sound repeated
over & over & over
i eat well
i exercise
i buy books about mermaids
i write poems about the above event
i write poems about the poems about the above event

re: vandals

for luke kennard

in an earlier draft of vandals
which appeared on stone 9th october 1757
i wrote 'thank you cara delevingne
luke kennard raymond roussel'
but later substituted luke kennard for selena gomez
don't ask why that is just the way it is
both luke kennard & selena gomez have so much to offer
both luke kennard & selena gomez are beautiful & strange human beings
but in the end it made more or less sense with her name
by way of apology i'm dedicating this poem to luke kennard

princess leia

i don't like you & i don't like you personally

— carrie fisher to paul simon

a phone vibrates in hell
today a last chance to smash up the benz
sketch unexpected changes to the prayer
they might not have laughed because it was funny
they might have laughed because they were uncomfortable
they must not laugh in church
in the golden toadstool i found revolting references to pop culture
george lucas removed princess leia's star
a long time ago, in a galaxy far far away
duran duran were taken seriously

for hmm the bell tolls

what a time to be alive
you with your cuddly toys glitter & gifts
hiding in a golden toadstool in the desert
where they are building a monument to you
i completely understand why the frog wants to spit
now seems the perfect moment to confess my indifference
to the texts you send to the poems you share
now seems the perfect moment to explain i am done
i am gone & just like justin's song
i'll be moving on
and you should go and love yourself

take a bow

wherever you go on chrome yr only a stone's throw
from a bunch of idiots
talking don delillo
the same joke repeated over & over & over
on any street corner older than rome
a bunch of idiots talking spoons
as if they've seen the inside of a spoon
what is worse: they write
what is worse: i am in a toadstool with toothpaste
a spoon rolls down the flume
vandals weep in the ashes of the supermarket
ideas take on meanings different to the those they once subscribed
thank you frank thank you luke thank you cara & selena
take a bow
toss your whipped cream in the sink
drink pink mink
take a long walk from a short plank
embrace the mace suck it up spit it out
we hope you enjoyed the show
there will be no refunds

vi. fuck these mutherfuckers

the new insincerity

there is not much in poetry that remains unsaid
but that you should say it is not your responsibility

neal astley made me scrabbled eggs for breakfast

neal astley made me scrabbled eggs
& asked me if i wanted a bloodaxe

what's a bloodaxe, i asked neal

be careful with the words you use
especially when you're insulting

seventeen tonnes of whale meat
under the bonnet of my white ferrari

do you want more egg asked neil

a bottle of water please
i'd rather be seen dead.

baby i don't care

i wasted the best years of my life
making breakfast for chelsey minnis, making lunch
for chelsey minnis
making dinner for chelsey minnis
while she wrote poetry
she was as pink as most people who are pink
she threw a cabbage at me
for coming home late from the store
she threw a turkey at me
for buying the cheapest beer in the store
& tossed it down the sink
i had a handful of dreams
i hid them from chelsey minnis until the day they came true
those were the best years of my life
the last thing i want is sympathy

white guilt

my first instinct is to destroy the poet
venom dripping from the page
into silver loops mediterranean

torched dimensions: a flute of champagne tipped
onto the bonnet of frank o'hara's jaguar
joyriding round times square tits out

on christmas day under a strawberry beret
i will die of excess candyfloss, levitation, golf carts
to the face

my first instinct was wrong
my last chance is gone

phosphorescence

i am burning books. you do not
have any new ideas. i am your
idea. you are short on ideas. i
am your idea. it is pretty inside
your cave. your house is made of
carapace. you do not understand
me. you can only see me from a
narrow island where there are
no trees. your luggage is fatally
flawed. put it in the microwave.
you are happy i am writing
about you. your eyes are made
of phosphorescence. you are
not angelic. i am happy you are
writing about me. you are an
interesting man. your poems
are better than mine. i run faster
than you. your golden years are
behind you, adieu. i wish i could
comfort you. she does not fancy
you. i do not fancy you. you
fancy you. she used to fancy
you. you have a sexual interest
in asphodels. you're an old
model. you hate this. i will not
apologize.

diego maradona

compressed through indifference
fuck these mutherfuckers
bite the heads off the bears
toss your belongings to the atlantic
flick a v at the pilot   fucking idiot   can't even drown
nonchalance   exubérance   en permanence
diego maradona   stade de france
neon eyed delinquent   the ball at his feet
the show about to begin
light work   seventy million dollars
in the back of a cab
do you think through bars
we reach anywhere higher

your character is very good but it can also be very bad

for poppy cockburn

count the likes before you fry the fox in sesame oil
behold dialogue between a child refusing to grow up and a
responsible adult
&&& every colour inside you is nervous
&&& everything about you suggests negroni season
welcome to a century of complete misery
i sense something about you quite bad
it is your character
you nod and say get on with it
i came to America and you left – an arm outstretched like an ocean
in my fantasies the swans are smothering you
i hold the sunset above your mouth and gently bring it down to
your breasts
the night in black with the full moon above a black horse
stop talking
the swans are tired of collecting oranges from the pond
let's stay authentic
let's all back to the future
after dinner we've got mist coming down
we've got someone to undress
how strong! how marvellous! how brave!
can i use your bathroom to piss into your aquamarine bathtub?
hollywood is a very real place
just be yourself

pink mink

"i have nothing to say to marianne moore & she has nothing to say to me!"

– chelsey minnis

that is to say: razorblades & sequins swirling in sewage

coated in pink mink cut a line of coke

by the rink cut a triple axel to cat's

double footed landing, ouch

*

ouch, that is to say: is she the girl from the internet?

drake on rollerblades? undress me – it's chiffon babe

undress me i am prince soaked by viagra falls

unlace my gown nail me good fuck me hard with your shoe

*

that is to say: double screening wrestling w/ jasmine gray

double axel to sunburnt face i've nothing better to double

than championship playoffs i don't care for either team

but i do wonder

*

that is to say: canary blood rushing the wolves throat

lana del rey singing "my pussy tastes like pepsi cola"

does the doctor have pepper spray i wonder

who has burnt my pizza?

*

that is to say: i am in a state of perpetual decay

i can't stomach you anymore than i can stand you

& i can't stand me one bit

my stomach knots with the past

*

that is to say: poetry is a bitch it takes me

round the park like a poodle on a chain of lace

hey that's chiffon babe drink liquid zinc or tie a leather belt

around my throat & yank it

*

ouch, ouch, you got me, or to say:

your poetry is so pretty i want to lick your ear

celebrate by pissing in leather trousers from a great height

onto your wedding cake

*

that is to say: this has all been terribly dull

my friends are a bunch of cunts

jesus doesn't want you for a sunbeam

& i'm not that kind of girl

absolute gravity

words appear
   on the walls

great lakes strung from her fingers
builders vomiting multicoloured glitter over gravel
the grass bends back
lacing the ditches with dull green
from where we admire
ponds full of nothing

twins walk past the gates
desperate for contact with the dead
shadows hover over the sun

expanding patches of green
leave a scent on the lawn
the swing-set swinging

tigers in the lemon grass
dolly mix ice-cream
red roses blushing into onrushing day

she pulls the plug from the whirlpool   flips vertical
the moon holds her
    in the palm of his hand
the north winds moan   impotent gods
   flickering
wet   with   gravity
water lilies   despotic moths   unkind destiny

the sky is only green because we're locked in

acknowledgments

a big thank you to aaron kent for his vision and tireless dedication to broken sleep books, shout out to emma, rue and otis!

thank you to my many friends and enemies in poetry especially astra, angelo, anthony vahni, chrissy, cliff, diana & luca, golnoosh, hiromi, jack, james, jasmine, laia, lila, luke, lucy, liam, matt, poppy, rebecca, rupert, sarah, serge, stuart, steve, susannah, and zoë

thank you to the baylis family, who have put up with several loud impromptu poetry readings & other nonsense

thank you to mark mansfield for helpful suggestions on early drafts of the manuscript. i used his version of 'lose your illusion'

thank you to andrew taylor, the martin hannett figure behind the collection & to ella frears, mark waldron, tim murphy & jade cuttle, for editorial suggestions, some of your ideas were useful – the rest i threw away.

this book is dedicated to julia (y hola a sus amigas!)

some of the poems have appeared in the following journals, occasionally in alternative forms:

3 a.m. magazine, ambit, abridged, berlin lit, blackbox manifold, the cadaverine, the international times, the journal, the literateur, the london magazine, the lonely crowd, the lotus eater, m58, magma, the new statesman, noon, pinyon, porridge, the rialto, spoonfeed, stride, strix, vibe, welter, wildcourt, zin daily. thank you to the editors.

thank you to the arts council, for financial support and helping me believe in myself

finally, thank you to you the reader for even the smallest cursory glance at my book, it's a real pleasure to be read.

notes

lots of music, novels and poetry have influenced my writing, the following lines stand out as not from my hand:

'j e n   x' contains a line from alanis morrisette's 'ironic' from the album jagged little pill

for hmm the bell tolls contains a line from justin beiber's 'love yourself' from the album purpose (deluxe edition)

'stephanie says' contains elements of the velvet underground song of the same name

'lana dey rey' contains quotes from bob dylan & leonard cohen

vandals contains a line from 'everyday is like sunday', from morrissey's album viva hate

lay out your unrest.

Ingram Content Group UK Ltd.
Milton Keynes UK
UKHW010605060623
422945UK00005B/190

9 781915 760180